# Gooney Bird
# and All Her Charms

# Gooney Bird and All Her Charms

by
## LOIS LOWRY

Illustrations by Middy Thomas

HOUGHTON MIFFLIN HARCOURT
Boston   New York

www.hmhco.com

The text of this book is set in Garamond.

The Library of Congress has cataloged the hardcover edition as follows:
Lowry, Lois.
Gooney Bird and all her charms / by Lois Lowry ; illustrated by Middy Thomas.
p. cm.
Summary: Gooney Bird's Great-Uncle Walter lends her second grade class a skeleton while they study human anatomy, and at the end of the month the students use Gooney Bird's charm bracelet to present all they have learned.
[1. Human anatomy—Fiction. 2. Skeleton—Fiction. 3. Schools—Fiction. 4. Charm bracelets—Fiction.] I. Thomas, Middy Chilman, 1931– ill. II. Title.
PZ7.L9673Gnd 2014
[Fic]—dc23
2012041887

ISBN: 978-0-544-11354-1 hardcover
ISBN: 978-0-544-45596-2 paperback

Printed in the United States
DOC 10 9 8 7 6 5 4 3 2

4500621223

*For Shira*

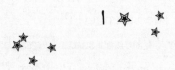

"It's March!" Mrs. Pidgeon said as she wrote the day's date on the chalkboard. "In like a lion, out like a lamb!"

She turned around and asked her second grade class, "Anyone know what that means?"

The children all looked puzzled. Then Nicholas's hand shot up.

"Nicholas?" Mrs. Pidgeon said.

"Ah, it means that, well, lions come in from the desert, and then—"

"Lions don't live in the desert!" Tyrone called out. "They live in the jungle!"

"No," Barry said in his professor's voice, "lions live on the Serengeti Plain."

"Whatever," Chelsea said. "*Tigers* live in the jungle! Isn't that right, Mrs. Pidgeon?"

Mrs. Pidgeon sighed.

"And what about those lambs?" Tyrone added. "Lions would just *eat* lambs. They'd have a big lamb stew for dinner!"

"So would tigers!" said Chelsea. "They'd pig out on lamb!"

"No, they'd *lamb* out! Munch munch munch." Tyrone moved his mouth ferociously. "Then they'd just spit the bones on the ground."

Keiko gasped and covered her ears. "Oh," she murmured, "please don't talk about that!"

"We won't, Keiko," Mrs. Pidgeon said. She went to Keiko's desk and gently took her hands away from her ears.

"Actually, class, I was quoting a saying that has to do with the weather." She went back to the board and pointed to the date. "It's March first today, and it's very cold outside. It's often cold at the beginning of March. Sometimes even snowy or icy. So the saying means that the beginning of March can be very *fierce*, like a . . . what?"

"Tiger?" said Chelsea.

"Rhino?" suggested Nicholas.

Felicia Ann timidly raised her hand. Mrs. Pidgeon nodded toward her. "Lion," she said in her soft voice. "It means that the beginning of March is very fierce, like a lion. But the end of March is like a lamb. *Gentle*."

"Good! Thank you, Felicia Ann," the teacher said.

Malcolm began to sing loudly. *"Mary had a little lamb, little lamb, little lamb . . ."*

Mrs. Pidgeon put her hand firmly on his shoulder. "Enough for now, Malcolm. We'll do some singing later today."

Malcolm stopped singing and slouched in his seat with a scowl.

"Grumpy face, grumpy face," Nicholas teased in a singsong voice.

"EVERYONE!" Gooney Bird said loudly. "I have an announcement." The students all fell silent. They looked at her. Every day there was something unusual about Gooney Bird. Sometimes it was quite startling, like the day she had worn a feathered hat and elbow-length black gloves to class; sometimes it was something very small, like the rhinestone earrings that she had described as "tiny, but tasteful."

Today Gooney Bird's clothes were fairly ordinary, at least for Gooney Bird. She was wearing black leggings under plaid Bermuda shorts, and a sweatshirt that said HUMPTY DUMPTY WAS PUSHED across her chest. On one wrist she wore a silver bracelet jingling with charms. The children all loved Gooney Bird's charm bracelet, which she had bought at a yard sale. ("Fifty cents!" she had told them. "And it's real silver!") From the bracelet dangled a tiny pair of sneakers, a little rocking chair, a basketball, a pair of spectacles, a miniature Volkswagen, a lobster, a wineglass, a pipe, a book, a slice of silver pizza, and—surprisingly—a skull.

Sometimes the second-graders had tried to make up stories about the charm bracelet. They had created a story about a marathon runner who finished his race, wearing sneakers, and then drove in his VW to a pizza parlor. They had created a different story about a lady who sat rocking while she read a book and a lobster crawled across the floor and grabbed her foot.

But none of the children quite knew how to work the skull into a story. The skull was spooky. Felicia Ann had suggested that Gooney Bird detach the skull from her bracelet but Gooney Bird thought that was not a good idea. "Someone created this bracelet," she said, "and each thing had a special meaning to that person. It wouldn't be fair to take anything away. We'll figure out what the skull means. It will just take time."

She always removed the bracelet and kept it inside her desk during the school day because the jingling of the charms made it hard for the children to pay attention to their work. But today the day was just starting and Gooney Bird was still jingling.

"Does your announcement have to do with what we are talking about, Gooney Bird?" asked Mrs. Pidgeon.

Gooney Bird thought for a moment. "It doesn't have to do with lions or lambs. And it doesn't have to do with weather. But it has to do with March, and with school, and with what we are going to study in March."

"Human body!" shouted Tyrone.

"Human body!" called Chelsea.

All of the second-graders joined in. "Human body! Human body!" they called.

Mrs. Pidgeon laughed. "I don't think you need to make an announcement, Gooney Bird," she said. "Everyone remembers what's on our schedule. So we'll turn to that section in our science books right now. Page fifty-two, class."

All of the children began to turn the pages to the section that was called "The Human Body." They had already completed the sections called "Weather" and "Insects" and "Engines."

"But, Mrs. Pidgeon, I think I'd better make my announcement right away. Otherwise you won't be prepared and it might come as a terrible surprise."

"What might come as a terrible surprise, Gooney Bird?" Mrs. Pidgeon asked. She had gone to the side of the room and was pulling down a large chart that had been rolled up like a window shade. The children, watching, could see two feet appear at the bottom of the chart, then the legs, until gradually the whole outlined body was there. At its top was the smiling face of a child.

"Yikes! I wouldn't be smiling if my whole insides were showing!" Beanie said.

"What's that big yucky blobby thing?" Malcolm asked, making a face. He pointed to the middle section of the child's body.

"I think maybe he ate an enormous mushroom," Keiko murmured. "At my parents' grocery store we sometimes have mushrooms that look like that."

"No, he ate a giant burger," Barry suggested.

"A Triple Whopper," Tyrone said.

"Gross," Beanie said.

"But if you ate a mushroom or a burger, it would be all chewed up. It wouldn't be a huge blobby lump like that," Nicholas pointed out. "It would be moosh."

"I don't think I'm going to like 'The Human Body,'" Felicia Ann whispered. "Not the insides, anyway."

"I really think I ought to make my announcement," Gooney Bird said in a very loud voice. "And by the way, that big blobby thing isn't something the guy ate. It's his liver."

"You're absolutely right, Gooney Bird,"

Mrs. Pidgeon said. "Good for you! Have you been studying the human body already?"

"Sort of. I always turn to it in our encyclopedia at home. And I've been thinking about it a lot because I knew we were going to be studying it in science, and because—well, this is my important announcement—"

But she was interrupted. The intercom speaker made a sudden buzzing sound. The class looked startled. Mr. Leroy, the principal, had already done the morning announcements, and Monroe Zabriskie, a sixth-grader, had led the Pledge of Allegiance.

"Mrs. Pidgeon?" They recognized Mr. Leroy's voice over the speaker.

"Yes?"

"We have a guest here who says he is delivering a gift for your classroom."

"A gift?" Mrs. Pidgeon looked puzzled. "I'm not expecting anything."

The children could hear Mr. Leroy laugh. "Well, it's quite a large box. And it looks heavy!

I'd bring it down myself but I'm not sure I could manage. Your guest— Just a minute."

They could hear the principal talking to someone else. "Your name again?" they heard him ask. Then he returned to his microphone. "Your guest, Dr. Walter Oglethorpe, says he's happy to deliver it to the classroom. Shall I send him down?"

"Well, I suppose so," Mrs. Pidgeon said in a confused voice.

"All right. He'll be there shortly." They could hear Mr. Leroy click the microphone off.

"Gooney Bird?" Mrs. Pidgeon said. "Does this have something to do with the important announcement you were trying to make?"

Gooney Bird nodded.

"And this person—Dr. Walter Oglethorpe? He is—?"

"My Uncle Walter. Actually, he's my mother's uncle."

"That makes him your Great-Uncle Walter."

"Right. My Great-Uncle Walter. He's a professor at the medical school."

"And he has a gift for us? In a large box?"

Gooney Bird nodded. "Don't freak out," she said.

"What is it? And why is he bringing it?" asked Mrs. Pidgeon. She went to the closed classroom door and looked through its window.

Gooney Bird sighed. "It will be very educational. And he doesn't need it right now so we can borrow it. And it's connected to what we're studying."

"'THE HUMAN BODY'! HE'S BRING-ING US A HUMAN BODY!" Chelsea shouted.

"Don't be silly, Chelsea," Mrs. Pidgeon said. "Here he comes." She opened the door.

"Please don't freak out, anyone!" Gooney Bird said to the class.

Keiko and Felicia Ann had both covered their eyes. Malcolm was standing up at his desk and flapping his hands the way he always did when he was nervous or excited. The class was whispering and giggling, but everyone fell completely silent when a tall, balding man entered, awkwardly carrying a very long, narrow box.

"Coffin," announced Barry in an awed voice. "It's a coffin!"

The man smiled and looked at Barry. "Good guess, young man," he said. "But not quite."

2

Dr. Oglethorpe set his large carton on the floor at the front of the classroom.

"Whew," he said. "That was heavy." Then he turned and shook hands with Mrs. Pidgeon.

"Good morning," he said politely. "You must be Gooney Bird's teacher."

She nodded. "Gooney Bird?" she said. "Will you introduce your great-uncle, please?"

Gooney Bird stood and came to the front of the room. "Class," she said politely, "this is my Great-Uncle Walter. His real name is Walter Eugene Oglethorpe. He is a doctor so you should all call him Dr. Oglethorpe. Except

you, Mrs. Pidgeon. You can probably call him Walter since you are both grownups. And I can call him Uncle Walter. But everyone else should call him Dr. Oglethorpe, okay?"

"Okay," the second-graders said. They were all staring at the box.

"Is that a dead body in there?" called Malcolm.

"Shhh," said Gooney Bird. "I haven't finished my introductions.

"Uncle Walter," she went on, "this is my teacher. We all call her Mrs. Pidgeon, but you can probably call her Patsy, because you both are grownups."

"Are you finished now?" Malcolm asked loudly. "Is that a dead—"

"Shhh," Gooney Bird said again.

"Class," Mrs. Pidgeon said, "let's use our good company manners. If anyone has a question for Dr. Oglethorpe, please raise your hand politely."

Every second-grader's hand shot into the air.

Dr. Oglethorpe looked at the children and the many raised hands. Then he pointed to Tricia.

"My mom is a doctor," Tricia said.

"That's nice," Gooney Bird's uncle said politely. "Did you have a question?"

Tricia looked flustered. "Uh, my mom is a dermatologist."

Malcolm and Barry were waving their hands wildly in the air.

"Well," said the doctor, "I am a professor of—"

"My mom's a nurse!" Tyrone called out.

"Nice," said Dr. Oglethorpe. He looked around the room. "Did you have a question, sweetie?" he asked Felicia Ann. "I think I saw your hand up a minute ago."

Felicia Ann's face turned pink. "I have a cat," she whispered.

"I have a Rottweiler!" called Tyrone.

"My mom had triplets!" Malcolm burst out.

"Goodness," said Dr. Oglethorpe.

Mrs. Pidgeon stepped forward. "Hands down, class," she said firmly. "It's getting late, and we haven't even started our science lesson, and I'm sure Dr. Oglethorpe has other things to do today. Doctor? I believe you brought us something related to our studies? Gooney Bird was going to explain but she never found the time."

Dr. Oglethorpe smiled. "Well," he said, "when Gooney Bird told her parents what you were about to start studying, and her mother told *me*, I realized I had something that might be a great help in your classroom. And I won't need it in *my* classroom—did I tell you that I am a professor of anatomy?—for a few weeks, so I've brought it for you to use for a little while."

He knelt down and began to unfasten the straps that held the lid tightly on the large box.

"What's anatomy?" asked Beanie.

"It's the study of the structure of an organism," Dr. Oglethorpe said.

"What's an organism?" asked Tricia, looking nervous.

The doctor unbuckled one strap. "Well, it could be a plant or an insect or an animal. But I am a professor of *human* anatomy. And Gooney Bird told me that you were about to begin studying the—"

"Human body!" Malcolm was flailing his arms. "Do you have a dead body in that box?"

Keiko closed her eyes tight and clapped her hands over her ears. "La la la la," she began to chant so that she wouldn't hear the answer.

"Very close!" Dr. Oglethorpe said. He unbuckled the last strap, leaned over the box, and lifted the contents out with a rattling sound.

The class gasped. Then they all said at once: "A skeleton!"

"Yup!" said Dr. Oglethorpe. He lifted it until its bony feet were touching the ground. It

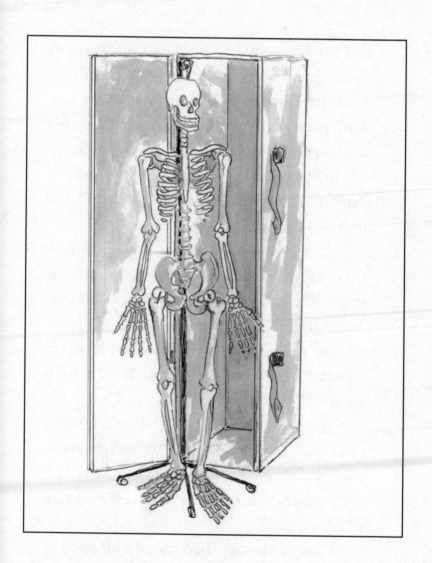

was as tall as he was. "Can you set up the stand, Gooney Bird?" he asked, indicating with his head that there was still something in the box. Mrs. Pidgeon helped her lift it out. They put the two parts together and stood it upright.

"My parakeet cage hangs from a stand like that!" Keiko said. She had removed her hands from her ears and opened her eyes again.

Dr. Oglethorpe attached the top of the skeleton to a hook on the stand. Then, carefully, he let go. The children began to applaud, and the doctor took a bow.

"Dr. Ooogle—? Dr. Ohgy—?" Malcolm sighed. "I can't say your name, but I have a question!"

"You can call me Dr. O.," Gooney Bird's great-uncle said with a smile. "What's the question?"

"How many bones does he have?" Malcolm asked.

"I know! I know!" Barry waved his hand in the air. "Two hundred and six!"

"Barry's a know-it-all," Chelsea announced.

"Well," Dr. Oglethorpe said, "he got it right. A human body does have two hundred and six bones. But if you try to count them on this skeleton, you won't find that many. Some bones are so very tiny that it would have been too hard to include them. So this guy"—he patted the side of the skeleton fondly, and the bones clattered a bit—"is missing a few tiny ones, mostly in his feet and hands. But he has the most important ones."

"Dr. O.! Dr. O.!" Beanie had a question. "What's his name?"

"A skeleton doesn't have a name, stupid!" Malcolm said.

"I am not stupid!" Beanie wailed. "I'm not, am I, Mrs. Pidgeon?"

"Of course not, Beanie," Mrs. Pidgeon said. "You came in first in the spelling bee last Friday, remember?" She patted Beanie's shoulder. "And, Malcolm, we do not use that word in this classroom, remember?"

"Actually," said the doctor, "he does have a name. My students gave it to him. They call him Napoleon. Can you guess why?"

The children all thought. But no one had an answer, except Mrs. Pidgeon, who was laughing. "I bet his whole name is Napoleon Bony-Part, right?" she said, and Dr. Oglethorpe nodded.

"Napoleon Bonaparte was a very famous French general," Mrs. Pidgeon explained to the class.

"We could call him Bony for short," suggested Ben.

"No," Gooney Bird said solemnly. "He shouldn't have a goofy name. We should be very respectful. He's a very distinguished skeleton." She stroked the long bone at the top of his left leg. Then she looked down and giggled a little. "He has big feet, though."

Dr. Oglethorpe picked up the empty box. "I must be off," he said. "But I know I'm leaving Napoleon in good hands. Just be careful with him. You can take him down from the stand and seat him in a chair if you wish. His joints work well. See?" He demonstrated the joints, bending Napoleon's left knee, then his right elbow. "His hip joint is really amazing. See this?" He pointed to Napoleon's hip. "It's a ball and socket. That's why we can move our legs in all directions. We wouldn't be able to dance if we didn't have this fabulous hip joint."

Chelsea, who took ballet lessons, stood on her tiptoes and lifted one leg out to the side.

Tyrone threw himself onto the floor beside his desk and did a few breakdancing moves.

Mrs. Pidgeon did a hopping little sort of jig.

"Good. You all have great hip joints! But be gentle with Napoleon. He doesn't have a layer of fat to pad his bones the way we do."

"I bet that's why he looks so skinny," Ben said.

"Dr. O.? Dr. O.?" Tricia had a question, and the doctor nodded to her.

"If Napoleon had all the rest of him, I mean

if he wasn't just bones, if he had fat, and—what else?"

"Muscles!" said Barry.

"Yes, if he had muscles and fat, and—skin?"

"Yes?"

"Would he be fat, or thin, or just medium?" Tricia asked.

"Good question," Dr. Oglethorpe said. "We have no way of knowing. Bones are the same in all people. We don't know if Napoleon was a fatty or a skinny, or—"

"Smart or dumb!" said Barry.

"Or Japanese?" suggested Keiko.

"African American?" said Tyrone.

"Or maybe he had bright red hair, like mine!" Gooney Bird pointed out.

Dr. Oglethorpe laughed. "Or perhaps he was a baldy, like me."

"Or had a beard, like my dad," suggested Ben.

"Could be," the doctor agreed. "We'll never

know." He patted Napoleon on the shoulder. "Goodbye, pal," he said. "Have a nice visit in second grade."

The class called a thank-you to Dr. Oglethorpe. Gooney Bird left the room to walk her great-uncle to the front door of the school. And Mrs. Pidgeon carefully moved the stand so that Napoleon was next to the large chart that she had pulled down. They all stared at him quietly.

"See how his ribs protect the softer inside parts?" Mrs. Pidgeon pointed out.

"My dad broke two ribs once," Ben said. "He was hiking and he slipped on a wet place and fell into a big rock. It really hurt."

"But look!" Barry said, pointing to the chart. "If your dad didn't hit his ribs, he would have broken his heart, maybe! Or his lungs!"

"Good for those ribs!" Mrs. Pidgeon said. "Is your dad okay, Ben?"

Ben nodded. "He's fine. All healed."

"The skeleton protected his important organs," Mrs. Pidgeon said. "And it also made it possible for him to stand up and hike. Look at his strong leg bones. If we didn't have bones, well . . ." She stared at the skeleton for a moment.

Felicia Ann finished the sentence in an awed voice: "We'd just be a blob."

All of the children stared at Napoleon. They looked down at their own arms and legs.

"Blobs," they agreed.

"Look at Napoleon's head!" said Chelsea, suddenly.

"He's got pretty good teeth," Tricia said. "I bet he flossed."

"His eyeholes are kind of creepy," Tyrone pointed out. Then he chanted, *"Got two big holes in the front of my head, and got no eyeballs cuz I be dead . . ."* Tyrone was very good at creating rhymes and raps.

"I *meant*," Chelsea said impatiently, "does it remind you of anything?"

"A skull," Barry said.

"Yeah, a skull," Nicholas agreed. "It reminds me of a skull because it *is* a skull!"

"It reminds me of Gooney Bird's bracelet!" Keiko said.

"Yes! It's like the skull on Gooney Bird's bracelet!" Beanie agreed.

"Did I hear someone say my name?" The classroom door opened and Gooney Bird reappeared. "I brought Mr. Leroy back with me," she said. "He wanted to know what was in Uncle Walter's box."

The principal came through the door behind Gooney Bird. "It looked as if your class was receiving a good-size present! I thought I'd come see what it was. Gooney Bird wouldn't tell me. She said it should be a surprise."

"Look!" The second-graders pointed to the side of the room where the skeleton was dangling from his stand. Mr. Leroy turned, looked, and jumped back in surprise.

"Holy moley!" he gasped. "What on *earth*—?"

"It's Napoleon!" they called, laughing at his reaction.

"You might as well shake his hand," Mrs. Pidgeon told the principal. "He's going to be with us all month."

Mr. Leroy took a deep breath. Then he lifted Napoleon's bony hand and shook it gently. "Welcome to Watertower Elementary School," he said, and bowed slightly.

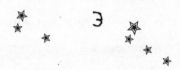

3

"Good morning, students," Mr. Leroy said on the intercom the next day after the bell rang and school had begun. "We have some announcements, and then a special treat this morning."

"I bet he's going to tell about Napoleon!" Barry said. "The other grades are going to be so jealous!"

"Shhh," said Mrs. Pidgeon. "Pay attention."

"First of all, good news," Mr. Leroy announced. "Bruno is home from the hospital and he's going to be fine!"

Everyone cheered. Bruno was the school

dog, a huge Newfoundland that belonged to Mr. Furillo, the school custodian. He slept most of the time, and everyone was accustomed to walking around a snoring pile of black fur. But poor Bruno. Last week he had fallen asleep beside the rear wheel of one of the school buses. His tail had been run over.

"Bruno will be back in school tomorrow and we'll all be happy to see him," Mr. Leroy went on. "No dog treats, though, please. And no lunch scraps! The vet said that Bruno is a little overweight. I think some of you have been giving him your sandwiches at lunchtime."

"Not the bread," Nicholas said in a loud whisper. "I just gave him the bologna."

"Shhh. Pay attention to Mr. Leroy." Mrs. Pidgeon put her finger to her lips.

"Next: remind your parents. Bake sale at lunchtime next Tuesday! We're all hoping that someone's mom will make those delicious lemon squares again! The proceeds will go toward new music for the school band, and our music director, Mr. Bornstein, says thank you in advance!"

"Now he's going to say about Napoleon, I bet!" Malcolm said.

"Shhh."

But he didn't. Instead, Mr. Leroy said, "Finally, our special treat this morning: Lielit Brehanu is going to lead us in the Pledge of Allegiance. Lielit's mother and father have just officially become American citizens!"

Everyone clapped. They all liked the quiet fourth grade girl who had come with her parents from Ethiopia last year. The children stood beside their desks and repeated the pledge with Lielit, who said the words proudly but sounded a little nervous over the intercom.

"Thank you, Lielit. And have a good day, everybody!" Mr. Leroy said, as he did every morning, and the speaker fell silent.

"I bet Napoleon's feelings are hurt," Beanie said. "He didn't even get *mentioned!*"

They all looked sympathetically at the skeleton.

"I'm starting to have an idea," Gooney Bird announced.

"What sort of idea?" Mrs. Pidgeon asked. They all knew that Gooney Bird's ideas were always good ones.

"About how we can make Napoleon famous in our school, but also it will be educational, and it won't be dangerous or anything."

"Sounds terrific," Mrs. Pidgeon said. "Ready to tell us about it?"

"Not quite. My brain is still at work."

"Fair enough. And actually, class, I was going to start our study of the human body with exactly that!"

"With what?" the children asked.

"With the brain!" Mrs. Pidgeon announced.

Keiko raised her hand and Mrs. Pidgeon said, "Yes, Keiko?"

"Napoleon doesn't have a brain," Keiko said sadly in a soft voice.

"He did *once!*" Barry said.

"Yes, he certainly did. And what protected it?" Mrs. Pidgeon used her pointer and pointed to the chart, where the outlined head showed a wrinkled pinkish brain. Then she pointed to Napoleon's head.

"Skull!" all the children called.

Gooney Bird reached into her desk and pulled out her bracelet. She held it up so they could all see the small silver skull.

"Mrs. Pidgeon! Mrs. Pidgeon!" Malcolm was waving his hand. "Guess what!"

"What, Malcolm?"

"Last summer, at Little League, the pitcher hit me in the head with the ball! But I had a helmet on, and under my helmet was my skull, so I had lots of protection, and my brain was okay!"

"I'm glad to hear that, Malcolm. Not glad that you got hit by the ball, but glad that you didn't get hurt. Now, class—"

"He did it on purpose! It was Jamie Morrissy

who was pitching, and he always hits people on purpose! My dad said that if he does it again—"

Mrs. Pidgeon went to Malcolm and put her calm-down arm across his shoulders.

"Malcolm's brain is at work right now, class," she said. "He's remembering last summer, and it is our brain that stores our memories."

"Lielit used her brain to remember all the words to the Pledge of Allegiance," Felicia Ann said.

"And to say them," Mrs. Pidgeon added. "Our brains control talking, and—what else?"

"Seeing!"

"Smelling!"

"Hearing!"

Every child had a hand in the air.

"The brain is like Command Central," Mrs. Pidgeon said. "Messages zoom around brain cells faster than we can even imagine. And we have billions of brain cells! They're called *neurons*.

"They tell us if we're hungry or thirsty, or if we hear an airplane—"

"Our ears tell us that!" Ben said.

Mrs. Pidgeon used her pointer and tapped on the left ear of the figure on the chart. "Correct. Our ears take in the vibrations that cause the sound, and then the inner parts of the ear process the vibrations and send them to the brain so that Command Central can decide what the sound is. A jet engine? A mosquito? A baby crying?"

"*Triplets* all crying at once!" Malcolm said, and put his hands over his ears.

"And if the brain tells you it's a jet flying over, it also tells you to—"

"Look up at the sky?" said Nicholas.

"Right. But if the brain says, 'Mosquito zooming in'?"

"Then Command Central says to slap it!"

Beanie said. The children all slapped at their own arms and necks.

"Right. The brain tells your muscles to move your arm into a slapping position."

"Never fast enough," Tricia said. Everyone laughed.

"Let's begin reading this chapter. Tyrone? Will you read the first paragraph aloud?"

Mrs. Pidgeon paused and looked at Gooney Bird. "Gooney Bird? You with us? Or is your brain still working on its idea?"

Gooney Bird looked up. "Nope," she said. "My idea is all worked out."

"Tell us! Tell us!" all the second-graders called.

"I will," she said, "after we read about the brain. Go ahead with your turn, Tyrone. Is your brain making a rap?"

Tyrone grinned. "Tryin' to," he admitted. "But I always tell it to stop when we're workin' on serious stuff."

He stood and began to read aloud as the other children followed the words in the book.

They took turns. Tyrone stood beside his desk and read about how important the brain was, and how it never stopped working, not even when you were asleep.

"I think it makes dreams," Felicia Ann whispered.

"And nightmares?" asked Keiko nervously.

"Yes, nightmares too."

"Oh dear," said Keiko.

"Why don't you go next, Keiko?" Mrs. Pidgeon suggested.

So Keiko stood and read about how the eyes are connected to the brain, and the brain explains to us what we are seeing.

Then Malcolm read to the class the paragraph about hearing. He still wanted to tell the class about the noise the triplets in his family made. All that screaming, Malcolm described, came in through your ears as vibrations, and if there were too many vibrations, and therefore too much noise, the person whose brain was hearing it might get a terrible headache.

"My mom always has a headache," he said.

"But sometimes those babies are laughing, Malcolm," Mrs. Pidgeon pointed out. "Does your mom have a headache then?"

"Well, no," Malcolm admitted. "She starts to laugh. We all do."

One by one the children stood and read aloud about the many things that the brain can do. When Chelsea read about the sense of smell, they held up different things that had different smells: an eraser, a jar of paste, an open marking pen, and an orange from Ben's lunch. They read about taste.

"The brain has to work *hard*," Barry said.

"And it has to remember everything!" Chelsea pointed out. "It has to *memorize!*"

"It's how we learn, isn't it, Mrs. Pidgeon? With our brains?" Tyrone asked. His foot began to tap a bit. He snapped the fingers on one hand.

Mrs. Pidgeon started to laugh a little. "Tyrone, I can tell that your brain is at work. You have a rap coming on, don't you?"

He nodded, with a grin.

"Okay, let's hear it," she said.

Tyrone stood, snapped his fingers, wiggled his hips, and chanted, *"Stuffing it full don't cause no pain, cuz that be the job of Mister Brain!*

"Lemme hear it!" he called to the class. *"Mister Brain!"* they all chanted.

Tyrone twirled in a circle and began his next verse. *"That noise you hear, is it a car or a train? Who knows the difference?"* He cupped his ear with his hand as if to listen.

*"Mister Brain!"*

*"You eat fried clams, or you eat chow mein?"* Tyrone twirled again and made an eating motion as if he were lifting a fork to his mouth. *"Who knows the difference?"*

*"MISTER BRAIN!"* the second-graders called loudly, laughing.

Tyrone bowed, and they all applauded. "I got more," he said. "But I'll save it."

"Save it in your brain!" Gooney Bird said. "And my brain's ready now with my idea."

The class was silent, waiting.

"We need to take Napoleon traveling," Gooney Bird said, "so that the other classes can meet him and learn about him."

"Traveling?" Chelsea said. "How can he travel?"

Gooney Bird pointed out the small wheels that allowed Napoleon's stand to move. "We roll him to his destination," she explained. "Then we'll lift him down and put him in his place. Remember Uncle Walter said we could sit him in a chair if we were careful?"

"What place? Where are we taking him?" Barry asked.

"You look worried, Barry," Gooney Bird said. "But look at Napoleon. He's not worried at all."

It was true. "He's smiling," Keiko said. All of the children stared at Napoleon's head. They made big smiles, showing their teeth.

"As for where we're taking him? We've been studying his brain. So we need to show him *using* his brain. Where would that be, in this school?"

Mrs. Pidgeon smiled. "I know!" she said. "The library! Of course," she added, "I hope you all use your brains *everywhere*. But I bet anything the library is what Gooney Bird has in mind."

Gooney Bird nodded.

"Gooney Bird," Mrs. Pidgeon went on, "I think you should go consult with Mrs. Clancy to be sure it's all right with her."

Gooney Bird was already at her cubby, looking for the hat that she always wore when she paid a call on someone important. And Mrs. Clancy, the school librarian, was certainly important.

"While I'm gone," Gooney Bird suggested,

"maybe you could think about how Napoleon should be dressed in a brain-using outfit for his visit to the library."

She adjusted the flowered hat over her red hair, left the classroom, and disappeared down the hall.

*"Dressed?"* said Mrs. Pidgeon, turning to the class. *"Brain-using outfit?* Oh, dear."

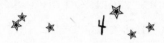

Barry and Ben, who had lifted Napoleon very carefully from his stand, sat him down in the chair that the class had selected. The library was filled with tables and chairs, but it also had a cozy reading corner furnished with a soft couch and a comfortable rocking chair. Sometimes Mr. Leroy sat there and read the newspaper in the middle of the morning, but not very often. He really liked drinking coffee with the newspaper, and Mrs. Clancy said, "Absolutely not. No coffee in the library." She let Mr. Leroy take the newspaper to his office, instead.

"Yes, that one's fine," Mrs. Clancy agreed

when the second-graders pointed out the rocking chair they had chosen for Napoleon. "I think he'd look very contented there. Let's give him a cushion." She took a soft pillow from the corner of the couch and placed it on the seat of the rocker.

Napoleon's ball-and-socket hip joints allowed his legs to bend at the hips so that he could sit with ease on the cushion. Then Ben bent one leg at the knee joint so that Napoleon's foot rested on the ground. Gently Tricia and Chelsea lifted his other leg, bent the knee, and rested his ankle across the opposite leg.

"That's exactly how Mr. Leroy sits in that chair," Mrs. Clancy said. "When I let him sit there," she added. "When he doesn't have a cup of coffee."

Napoleon's spine leaned against the back of the chair, and each arm, bent at the elbow joint, rested on a wooden chair arm.

"Look, Mrs. Pidgeon!" Malcolm stroked

the long bone of Napoleon's upper right arm. "Do you find this *humerus?*"

Mrs. Pidgeon groaned at the joke. She had explained to the children that the human arm had this one oddly named bone. "Yes, very *humerus,* Malcolm," she said with a laugh.

"We need to show him using his brain," Gooney Bird said. "So he should be reading something *really hard.*"

"How about this?" the librarian asked. "It couldn't be more appropriate. Mr. Furillo just returned it. He loves history, but he said this was pretty tough going." She went to her desk, held up a book, and read the title aloud. "*The Rise of Napoleon Bonaparte.*"

"He wouldn't be reading about *himself!*" Malcolm said loudly. "That's dumb!"

"But, Malcolm," Mrs. Pidgeon said, "if there were a book in this library called *Malcolm: The Difficult Life of an Eight-Year-Old Boy with Triplets at Home,* don't you think you would read it?"

"Yeah, I guess," Malcolm admitted.

"Well, duh!" said Chelsea.

"I always look up *Laysan albatross* when I come across a book about seabirds," Gooney Bird said, "because you know what their *other* name is!"

"Gooney bird!" the second-graders all said, laughing.

"I think we should let Napoleon read about himself," Mrs. Pidgeon said. She took the thick book from Mrs. Clancy and looked at it. "Even though it is six hundred and four pages long!"

Mrs. Pidgeon placed the book, open, on the skeleton's lap. Beanie and Tricia carefully arranged Napoleon's hands on the book.

"Look," said Beanie placing Napoleon's thumb and forefinger around a page, "he's just turning from page three forty-seven to three forty-eight."

"It's going to take him forever to finish that book!" Tyrone said.

"Maybe he's a really fast reader, like me!" Keiko suggested.

"He'd better be," Gooney Bird said, "because he only gets a few days in the library. Then we have to move him to his next spot."

"What's his next spot?" her classmates asked.

"Depends what body part we study next. That's up to Mrs. Pidgeon."

"We still have work to do here, class," Mrs. Pidgeon said. "We have to dress Napoleon in his brain-using outfit. Gooney Bird? You first."

Gooney Bird reached into her pocket and pulled out a pair of glasses. Gooney Bird kept many pairs of glasses in her cubby. She bought them at yard sales. She didn't *need* glasses — her vision was perfect, she said, 20/20 — but she liked to wear them occasionally. She felt that they made her look interesting, intellectual, and sophisticated.

The ones she had chosen for Napoleon's

stay in the library were large and round, with dark frames. Carefully she placed them over his eye sockets. "Too bad he doesn't have ears or a nose," she said. "That would help." But she managed to adjust the glasses on the skull, and when she took her hands away, they balanced there.

"Malcolm?" Gooney Bird said. "You're next. That will help."

Malcolm came forward and held up his furry green earmuffs. He stretched them apart, placed them on the skull, and when the metal connector tightened, they snapped in place over the earpieces of the glasses, holding them firmly.

They tilted the skull slightly so that Napoleon's skull was looking at the book that he held in his lap.

Gooney Bird frowned. "You know what? We talked about a brain-warming hat, but I don't think he needs one. He looks very brainy just like this."

"Studious," Mrs. Pidgeon commented.

"Attentive," said Mrs. Clancy.

"And a good reader," Keiko added.

"So: no hat," Gooney Bird said. "The only things left are the signs. Tyrone? Felicia Ann? How are you doing?" Gooney Bird looked toward the computer wall. Tyrone and Felicia Ann had been hard at work on two computers.

*"Napoleon's signs be almost done,"* Tyrone chanted. *"Me and Felicia Ann, we havin' fun!"*

Mr. Pidgeon went to the printer and looked at the pages of large print that had appeared one after another.

"Good job, guys!" she said. She handed the pages to the children. Mrs. Clancy found some Scotch tape in her desk.

First they taped a sign to the door of the school library.

COME MEET NAPOLEON
PLEASE BE QUIET

The next sign was taped to the table beside Napoleon's chair.

NAPOLEON IS USING HIS BRAIN.
IT IS INSIDE HIS SKULL.
HIS SKULL PROTECTS IT.

On another nearby table they taped another sign.

HIS BRAIN IS FULL OF NEURONS.
THEY SEND MESSAGES TO HIS OTHER PARTS.

Carefully they placed the third sign on the floor near Napoleon's foot.

HE IS READING.
HIS EYES ARE SEEING THE LETTERS AND SENDING THE MESSAGES TO HIS BRAIN.

"Where shall I put this one?" Keiko asked, holding a sign.

The children thought it over and decided to tape the next sign to the side of the chair. Keiko placed it there neatly.

HE IS WEARING EAR MUFFS
SO THAT VIBRATIONS WON'T ENTER HIS
BRAIN WHILE HE IS READING.
PLEASE BE QUIET IN THE LIBRARY!

"One more," Gooney Bird said. "I'll put this one here on the front of Mrs. Clancy's desk."

THE BRAIN ALSO SENDS MESSAGES
ABOUT SMELLING AND TASTING
AND PAIN AND DANGER AND HAPPINESS
AND MANY OTHER THINGS!
THE BRAIN IS VERY, VERY IMPORTANT!
BE CAREFUL NOT TO DAMAGE YOUR
BRAIN!

"What does that mean?" Malcolm asked. "How can you protect your brain from getting damaged?"

"You should know that, Malcolm," Beanie told him. "Wear a batting helmet!"

"Or a bike helmet!" Nicholas added.

"Or a seat belt!" Felicia Ann said. "And don't do drugs, either. Here. I brought you one more." She and Tyrone had turned their computers off and joined the other children. She handed the final sign to Gooney Bird.

Gooney Bird looked at it and laughed. She tore off a piece of tape, leaned down, and attached the last sign to Napoleon's left upper arm.

MRS. PIDGEON'S SECOND GRADE
FINDS THIS HUMERUS.

"Goodness," Mrs. Pidgeon said. "It's almost lunchtime. Have a nice stay in the li-

brary, Napoleon. We'll be back for you in a few days!"

The children all waved to Napoleon as they left the library. Napoleon didn't wave back. He was very busy using his brain to read.

5

"I don't know how you can stand to eat that, Malcolm," Gooney Bird said, looking at the pizza slice that Malcolm was folding into thirds. "It's not even interesting."

It was Thursday, and the school lunch on Thursday was always pizza. Malcolm took a bite of his, and then nibbled a dangling bit of cheese into his mouth.

"That's gross, Malcolm," Chelsea said. "I bet you slurp spaghetti, too."

Malcolm grinned. He made a loud slurping noise and Chelsea rolled her eyes.

"Anyway," Malcolm said, with his mouth

full, "food isn't supposed to be interesting. It's just supposed to taste good and fill you up."

"I disagree," Gooney Bird told him. "I think food should be nutritious, and filling, and delicious—"

"Right! And my pizza is all of those things!"

"Let me finish. And also it should be colorful to look at—"

"My pizza is! Look at it! Orange, mostly! And the pepperoni is sort of maroon!"

"I haven't finished. And it should also be *interesting.* That's why I always bring my lunch from home. Every single day I put something in my lunch that is from a foreign country. Usually for dessert. Yesterday I had a Brazil nut, remember?"

Malcolm nodded.

"And the day before that, a kumquat. And on Monday, a red banana."

Malcolm nodded again. He looked at the half slice of pizza that he was still holding. "My mom doesn't have time to make me an interesting lunch," he explained sadly. "Every morning she has to feed all three of the babies, and they throw stuff, and they smear oatmeal in their hair, and—"

Gooney Bird sighed. "Yeah," she said sympathetically. "It's hard. You know what? Finish your pizza while I finish my cucumber and hummus sandwich. Then I'll share my dessert with you."

Malcolm brightened. "What's your dessert?" he asked.

"Pomegranate," Gooney Bird told him.

"Oh. I was hoping you were going to say brownies."

"Brownies aren't *half* as colorful and interesting as pomegranate!"

Barry Tuckerman, who was seated near them in the multipurpose room where they were having lunch, was listening. He folded his napkin neatly into a rectangle and used it to brush the crumbs off the table onto the floor. Bruno, Mr. Furillo's Newfoundland, looked over from

his bed in the corner, raised himself to his feet, came over next to the table and licked up the crumbs, then returned to his bed. He wagged his bandaged tail slightly.

"Uh-oh," Beanie said. "We're not supposed to feed him. He's on a diet."

"It was only a few crumbs," Barry pointed out. "You know what?" He picked up a cookie and examined it. "It's nice to have an interesting lunch. And it's nice to have a colorful lunch. And it's important to have a nutritious lunch. You should have some salad with your pizza slice, Malcolm."

"Yeah, I will." Halfheartedly Malcolm poked his plastic fork into a little cup of coleslaw.

"But after you chew it all up, it doesn't matter if it's a red banana or a brownie or a kumquat or a whatever. Because after your teeth work on it, it's all just *moosh*." Barry took a quick bite of the cookie he was holding. He chewed it loudly, then stuck out his tongue. "MOOSH," he said. "See?"

Keiko, seated at the end of the table, whimpered and put her hands over her eyes. "Yuck," she whispered.

"It's true," Tricia said. "By the time it goes down the . . . the . . . What's it called? That tube it goes down?"

"Esophagus!" Barry, Beanie, and Tyrone all said it loudly together.

"Yes. Esophagus. It's just moosh when it goes down that into your stomach."

"Did I hear someone say *esophagus?*" Mrs. Pidgeon appeared at their table. "Does that mean you were all paying attention to our science lesson this morning?"

The children all laughed and nodded their heads.

"What happens to the food while you chew it?" she asked.

"It gets mixed with—?"

"Saliva!" they said together.

"And then it goes through the—?"

"Esophagus!"

"Into the—?"

"Stomach!"

"Right! Does everyone have a full stomach? Have you all finished your lunch?"

Bruno looked up as the children threw away their paper napkins, closed their lunchboxes, and returned their trays. His big brown eyes watched carefully to see if any more crumbs or scraps of food had fallen on the floor. Then, disappointed, he went back to sleep.

Gooney Bird looked around the multipurpose room as her class prepared to leave. The lunch ladies behind the counter were cleaning up and storing the leftover milk cartons in the big refrigerator. Mr. Furillo was standing in the doorway with his huge broom. Very soon, when all the classes had finished their lunch, the custodian would move the tables to the side and sweep the floor, Bruno following him in hope of crumbs.

"Mr. Furillo?" Gooney Bird said politely as she approached the door with the rest of her class. "I have a favor to ask."

He listened while she described her request. Then he nodded his head. "Gotcha," he said.

Walking back to the second grade classroom quietly, Gooney Bird spoke to Mrs. Pidgeon. "I know we have math this afternoon, and spelling, and recess, but . . ."

"But what?" Mrs. Pidgeon asked.

"Now that we've learned all about the digestive system," Gooney Bird said, "I think it's time for Napoleon to make a move."

Napoleon had been in the library now for four days. His glasses had become a little lopsided and his book was tilted, about to fall out of his hands. But he still looked like a guy using his brain.

Every classroom in Watertower Elementary School had been to visit him. Three kindergarten children had been frightened and cried, but most of the students had found Napoleon fascinating. One fourth grade boy, Philip Romano, who had trouble concentrating on schoolwork, announced that from now on he would wear ear muffs, as Napoleon did.

Sixth-grader Marlon Washington, who was often a troublemaker, announced at first that he thought Mrs. Pidgeon's second grade was just a bunch of babies acting like big shots because someone gave them a stupid skeleton. But after his class visited the library and Marlon examined Napoleon, he changed his mind. "That is one very cool dude," he said. "Look at him, using those neurons!"

Mr. Leroy did not allow any student to have a cell phone in school. But he did have one himself, and he agreed to take a picture of each child standing beside Napoleon. Some of the children tried to make a big toothy smile so that they would resemble the skull, but most looked very serious and solemn in their photographs.

One mother, Mrs. Gooch, wearing a hat and

gardenia perfume, came to the school to complain that having a skeleton in the library was disgusting. It was un-American, she said, like something they might do in a foreign school, maybe in Sweden or a place like that. Mr. Leroy told her that the skeleton was being used for educational purposes and that the children were learning valuable information about the human body. Mrs. Gooch said that her Veronica, a third-grader, was entirely too young to learn anything about the human body. Mr. Leroy listened politely to Mrs. Gooch and then agreed that Veronica could stay in her classroom and read a book while her classmates visited Napoleon, if that's what her mother wished. Mrs. Gooch said, "That is precisely what I wish!" in a meaningful voice and then went away, and Mr. Leroy sprayed air freshener in his office to get rid of the scent of her gardenia perfume.

The other children, all but Veronica Gooch, paid very careful attention to Napoleon and what they learned from him. But Mrs. Clancy, the librarian, said that not one single student understood the sign that read MRS. PIDGEON'S SECOND GRADE FINDS THIS HUMERUS. She had to explain it again and again, she reported, even to Mr. Leroy.

"Well, we have to educate them," Gooney Bird said. "Save that sign about the humerus, Tyrone," she said. "We can throw all the brain ones away because we have new ones for the digestive system."

Tricia and Beanie carefully removed Napoleon's glasses and earmuffs. Then Ben and Barry lifted the skeleton onto his rolling stand and prepared for his move. Gooney Bird held the door of the library open as the boys maneuvered the stand, with Napoleon, undressed and dangling, out of the library. In the doorway, Barry lifted the skeleton's arm and waved goodbye with it to Mrs. Clancy.

She grinned. "I find that humerus," she said.

# 6

"Where to?" Ben asked as they made their way down the hall.

"Multipurpose room," Gooney Bird instructed. "Mr. Furillo's waiting."

Tyrone and Felicia Ann remained in the library, at the computers, working on the next set of signs. Mrs. Pidgeon and the other second-graders all accompanied Napoleon on his journey past the classroom doors.

"I have his digestion clothes," Chelsea announced. She held up something neatly folded.

Mr. Furillo held the door for them as they

wheeled the stand inside. The large room was neatly swept as it was each day after lunch. The lunch ladies had gone home, and the kitchen area was tidy and clean. The trays were stacked.

"I did what you asked, Gooney Bird," the custodian told her. "Left one table out, and one chair. Over here in the corner."

Bruno, who had been sleeping, got up and ambled to the corner with them. When they got to the table and chair, Ben and Barry carefully unhooked Napoleon, lifted him from the stand, and sat him in the chair. It was easier this time than it had been in the library because they knew now just how his hip and knee joints worked.

The lunch chair had no arms, but when they pushed it in under the table, Napoleon's arms rested on the table and he looked quite comfortable. Gooney Bird went to the kitchen area and came back with a plate, fork, and napkin.

Chelsea began to dress Napoleon in his digestion clothes. First she put on his plaid bow tie. It was already tied, and snapped neatly around the skeleton's neck.

"It's my dad's," Chelsea explained. "My dad said that if Napoleon was going out for dinner, he should be dressed up and wearing a tie."

The children nodded. They all agreed. And with the bow tie at the base of his neck, below his chin, Napoleon did look quite formal.

"Now this," Chelsea said, and she unfolded a large paper bib. Across the bottom of the bib were the words CAP'N BILL'S SEAFOOD SHACK and a cartoon picture of a lobster.

"Don't cover up his bow tie!" Tricia said.

"I won't." Chelsea tied the bib onto Napoleon and arranged it carefully so that the bow tie appeared above it.

Gooney Bird placed a plate on the table in front of Napoleon and gently arranged his hands on either side. She put a fork between his right thumb and fingers. Then she spread the paper napkin across his lap.

"He needs something to drink," Ben said.

"I've got it," Mrs. Pidgeon said. She reached into her large purse and brought out a stemmed glass. She placed the glass on the table near Napoleon's right hand.

"I thought he should have a nice glass of wine with his dinner," she explained.

"Especially since he's wearing a bow tie. It's a pretty fancy occasion for him."

"Yeah, and he's old enough for wine," Malcolm said. "I think he's probably like a hundred."

"Maybe a hundred and ten," Nicholas said.

They all stood back and admired the scene. Bruno went to the table and sniffed.

"Oh, no!" Keiko said in an alarmed voice.

"What? There aren't any crumbs because there's no real food," Beanie reassured her.

"But Napoleon is—" Keiko hesitated. "I

don't want to say it in front of Bruno," she whispered.

"*What?*"

"He's *bones*," Keiko said in a very nervous voice.

All of the children looked startled. Even Mrs. Pidgeon cringed a little. "Oh dear," she said. "Mr. Furillo? What do you think?"

"Nah," Mr. Furillo reassured them. "I wouldn't trust him if you put real food on that dish. Like pizza, or a burger. If you turned your back he'd grab it. Remember that time a first-grader dropped his hot dog?"

"Jason. He's that kid with curly hair. I remember that. Bruno ate it in one gulp and Jason cried," Malcolm said. The other children nodded. They all remembered it. Jason had cried *loudly*.

"But look at him. He sniffed around, but nothing smelled good to him. He'll be okay. I'll keep an eye on him," Mr. Furillo said.

"I guess Bruno didn't find that humerus!" Gooney Bird said.

"Huh?" Mr. Furillo looked puzzled.

"Nothing. It's just a joke."

"Here come the signs!" Mrs. Pidgeon announced. Tyrone and Felicia Ann appeared with Mrs. Clancy, who had brought her tape dispenser.

The second grade went to work. In a very short time, all of the signs were taped neatly in place.

On the door to the multipurpose room, one read:

COME SEE NAPOLEON
DIGEST HIS DINNER!

On one side of the table where Napoleon was sitting, a sign read:

WHEN NAPOLEON CHEWS,
HIS FOOD GETS MIXED WITH SALIVA.

IT TURNS INTO MOOSH SO HE CAN SWAL-
LOW IT.


"Once I gave one of my triplets a chicken
nugget but he didn't know how to chew it,
and he choked," Malcolm said. "So my mom
grabbed him and turned him upside down and
thumped on his back, and the chicken flew out
onto the floor, and he was okay."

"What did your mom do to *you?*" Chelsea
asked.

"Well, she said she felt like turning me upside down and thumping on me, but she didn't."

"You learned a good lesson," Mrs. Pidgeon
said. "No more chicken until they're older,
right?"

Malcolm nodded. "Only moosh. That's all
they eat. Plus Cheerios."

The second sign read:


THE MOOSHED FOOD GOES
DOWN HIS ESOPHAGUS . . .

They taped that one to the other side of the table, and below it they taped the third sign:

. . . INTO HIS STOMACH. THERE IT GETS MOOSHED AROUND MORE. AND IT GOES NEXT TO . . . FOLLOW THE ARROW —>

"This part is so cool!" Ben said.

"I don't think so," Keiko replied, making a face. "I don't like this part."

The arrow on the sign pointed toward the wall of windows. On the floor below the windows, Mr. Furillo had carefully laid a long green garden hose. It extended from the corner of the room all the way along the side wall, halfway to the kitchen entrance. In the spring he would use it to water the shrubbery beside the front steps of the school. But now, in March, he didn't need the hose. It had been rolled up in his utility room until today.

On the windowsill above the hose, they taped the fourth sign:

NAPOLEON'S SMALL INTESTINE.
IT IS 20 FEET LONG.
INSIDE HIM, IT IS ALL CURLED UP
LIKE A SNAKE.

"I wish we didn't say the snake part," Keiko murmured.

Gooney Bird tried to make her feel better. "It's just like a garden snake," she told Keiko. "Harmless. Not a cobra or anything."

But Keiko still looked nervous. She felt her own abdomen with one hand.

"Look at the next sign!" Tyrone said excitedly. "Look! I made it rhyme!"

Sure enough. The next sign, on the next windowsill, said:

NUTRITIOUS STUFF GOES TO HIS BLOOD
AND SWIMS AROUND LIKE IN A FLOOD.

"Good rhyming, Tyrone!" Gooney Bird said.

"I could do a whole rap about the human body! I could teach you guys the moves!" Tyrone closed his eyes and moved his feet. *"The brain, and the blood, and the bones, and the . . ."*

"Not now, Tyrone." Mrs. Pidgeon put her hand on his shoulder. "Maybe on the playground, later. Let's look at the last sign now. You and Felicia Ann did such a good job!"

The final Digestive System sign was taped to the leg of Napoleon's chair.

THE LEFTOVERS GO TO HIS LARGE INTESTINE.
IT IS NOT AS LONG AS THE SMALL.
USELESS STUFF STAYS THERE
UNTIL NAPOLEON GOES TO THE BATH-ROOM AND GETS RID OF IT.

"Or until it ends up in your diapers! And *stinks!*" Malcolm said loudly. "Did I tell you about the time that—"

"Shhh. Yes, you have told us many times,

Malcolm. Your poor mom has to change a lot of diapers." Mrs. Pidgeon put her hand on Malcolm's shoulder. "You've done a great job, everyone! The other grades are going to learn a lot about the digestive system from Napoleon because of your hard work. Let's go now and let him enjoy his dinner in peace."

"Bye, Napoleon! Have a nice dinner!" the second-graders called as they filed out of the multipurpose room.

"Keep an eye on Bruno, Mr. Furillo," Goony Bird reminded the custodian.

"I will! I won't let him find that humerus!" Mr. Furillo chuckled. "I just got it," he said.

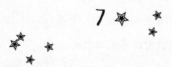

# 7

After a week of fine dining it was time for Napoleon to move again. But the second grade was having an argument.

"But it would be very educational!" Barry said.

"No!" wailed Keiko.

"And it would be funny!" Malcolm added.

"No!" said Felicia Ann and Beanie together.

They had been making their plans that day, at lunch in the multipurpose room. Gooney Bird had brought a small plastic container filled with marinated artichoke hearts, which she had passed around for each child to have a taste. "Not bad," they decided. She had brought, as well, a fresh artichoke, which she showed them. It was a strange-looking vegetable, and some of the children said "Ouch!" when they pricked their fingers on the sharp tips of its leaves.

When they were finished examining the artichoke, they placed it on Napoleon's plate. All of the classes had visited him and read the informational signs. Even Veronica Gooch had come, with her third grade class. But Mrs. Gooch had called the school this time to complain about the wineglass. It was un-American, she said, like something the French might do. So they had taken the wineglass away and given Napoleon a coffee cup instead.

But it was time now, they agreed, for Napoleon to move on. While they cleaned up their lunch remains, the second-graders talked about where he should go. It was then that Malcolm, returning from the bathroom, announced his idea: that Napoleon should be moved to the boys' room.

"We can sit him on the toilet!" Malcolm said excitedly. "In a stall! And when people come into the bathroom, they'll see *skeleton feet* under the door!"

All of the boys loved the idea.

"It's part of digestion, right, Mrs. Pidgeon? After the leftovers are in the large intestine, then—"

"Well, yes," she replied, "but—"

"It's gross!" Chelsea said loudly.

The other girls all agreed. None of them liked Malcolm's plan. The argument went on and on. It continued back in the classroom.

"I could make a whole rap about it! *Hey, Napoleon, he da man; he be sittin on da . . .*"

Tyrone was wiggling at his desk.

Mrs. Pidgeon interrupted him. "No," she said, firmly. "We are not sitting Napoleon on the toilet. And that's that. It might be educational. And it might be funny. But it would be sexist."

"Sexist? What does that mean?" Nicholas asked.

"It means not fair to one of the sexes."

"Huh?"

"For example, what if only women were allowed to be president of the United States? And no men allowed?"

"That wouldn't be fair! I want to be president when I grow up!" Barry said huffily.

"I might, also," Gooney Bird commented. "I haven't decided yet."

"I'd like to be *king*," Malcolm said.

"Good luck with that, Malcolm," Mrs. Pidgeon said. "Anyway: males and females are considered equal in this country. They have equal opportunities."

"So? What's wrong with our plan for Napoleon? What's sexist?" Ben asked. Then he thought for a moment. "Oh," he said. "I get it."

The other boys all got it too. "Oh," they said, one after another. "No girls would get to see him."

"Yeah," Barry said, in a disappointed voice. "It wouldn't be fair. We need to think of something *fair*."

"And," Gooney Bird pointed out, "it should demonstrate another body system. We did his brain. And we did digestion. Remember what we learned about next?" She lifted one arm.

Today she was wearing a short-sleeved white blouse and a man's necktie. She bent her arm and posed like a strongman.

"I find that humerus," Felicia Ann said, and giggled. The other children groaned.

"Muscles!" they all called.

"Right. Let's do his muscular system next. Doesn't that make sense, Mrs. Pidgeon?"

"It does!" the teacher agreed. "And of course we know where we should take him to demonstrate his muscles!"

"The gym!"

"Right. We'll move him there at the end of the school day, so he'll surprise everyone in the morning. Let's review what we know about muscles so that we can plan to make our signs. Who wants to tell me where our muscles are located, and what they do? Ben?"

"They're all over our skeleton, and they make our bones move," Ben said.

"Tendons attach them to our bones," Nicholas added.

"And they're stretchy, and rubbery!" Tricia said. "Like this!" She was holding a wide rubber band in both hands. She stretched it until her hands were far apart. "Ouch!" she said when the band snapped back.

"Right," Mrs. Pidgeon said. "Very stretchy. And they work in pairs. One muscle pulls and the other relaxes. So I can bend my arm, and then I can unbend it." She held up her arm and all the children imitated her. Together they bent and unbent their arms. "Tighten, relax. Tighten, relax.

"And please," she added, "I don't want to hear a single person say that they find this humerus!"

Malcolm began to whisper it, but everyone said, "Shhh." They were all tired of the humerus joke.

"Oh, *no!*" Barry said suddenly. He groaned, and put his head into his hands. Everyone was startled. They all looked at Barry. "I may throw up!" he wailed.

Mrs. Pidgeon rushed the large wastebasket to Barry's side. "Do you want to go to the nurse's office? What's wrong?"

After a moment Barry looked up. "My grandma and grandpa came to visit us this weekend," he said, "and we all went out to a fancy restaurant for dinner. My grandpa said we could have whatever we wanted. And he paid."

"Well, that's nice," Felicia Ann said. "I would get spaghetti."

"I'd get a cheeseburger," Tyrone said.

"Lobster!" Chelsea announced. "It's *very expensive!*"

"I think I'd have caviar," Gooney Bird announced. "I have never once had caviar. And I would wear a fur hat."

Barry looked stricken. He took a deep breath. Then he moaned, "I ate muscles."

"Yuck!" the second-graders responded. "You ate *muscles?*"

He nodded. "They were stretchy and rubbery," he told them. "And remember we learned that it takes up to three days for food to go through your digestive system? It was just Saturday night that I ate muscles."

Everyone fell silent. They were murmuring, "Saturday, Sunday, Monday . . ."

"Dude," Tyrone said in an ominous voice, "you may still have some muscles in there."

Mrs. Pidgeon was laughing. "Barry, Barry,

Barry," she said. "Look! Lift your head and look at the chalkboard!"

In big letters she wrote: *MUSCLES.* Then, beside it, she wrote: *MUSSELS.*

"Two different things! Sound the same, spelled differently," Mrs. Pidgeon explained.

"We'll learn more about mussels when we get to the 'Creatures of the Sea' chapter in our science book."

"Oh," said Barry, brightening. "Good. Actually, I liked them quite a bit."

"How shall we dress Napoleon for the gym?" Keiko asked. They had already removed his Digestive System outfit, the bow tie and the bib.

"Baseball cap!" called Malcolm. "Yankees!"

"Red Sox!" Ben said loudly. He was wearing a red shirt that said BIG PAPI on the back.

Mrs. Pidgeon, aware that a serious argument was about to develop, quickly went to the piano and played the opening chords to a song the whole class knew. *"Take me out to the ball game,"* the children began to sing. *"Take me out with the croooowd . . ."*

They were still singing bits and pieces of the song at the end of the school day when they wheeled Napoleon into the gym, but by then they had agreed that a gym was not a place for baseball. Carefully they lifted the skeleton from his stand and sat him on the floor leaning against the bottom row of the bleachers with a basketball wedged between his knees. On his bony feet were an enormous pair of bright green sneakers that they had borrowed from Mr. Goldman, the boys' gym teacher. And around his skull, across his forehead, was a sweatband.

Napoleon looked as if he was waiting for the coach to send him into the game.

The sign that Tyrone and Felicia Ann had made for the door of the gym read:

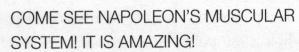

COME SEE NAPOLEON'S MUSCULAR
SYSTEM! IT IS AMAZING!

Taped to the bleacher seat beside Napoleon, another sign read:

HE HAS MORE THAN 600 MUSCLES!
THEY WORK IN PAIRS.
THEY MAKE HIS BONES MOVE.

A sign beside one of his green sneakers read:

HE HAS 26 BONES IN EACH FOOT! AND 27
IN EACH HAND!
BUT THEY WOULDN'T BE ABLE TO MOVE
WITHOUT HIS MUSCLES.

There was one more sign taped beside Napoleon's hip. It had an arrow pointing to Napoleon's behind. It read:

HE EXERCISES A LOT
SO HIS MUSCLES ARE STRONG.
HIS LARGEST MUSCLE IS IN
HIS BUTT.

Mrs. Pidgeon looked at that sign and frowned.

"I wonder if anyone might object to that one," she said.

"But it's *true,* Mrs. Pidgeon," Felicia Ann pointed out. "We read it in our science book."

"But the science book didn't use the word *butt,*" the teacher said. "Anybody remember what it said instead? I wish I'd brought the book with me."

"Maybe it said *bottom,*" Keiko suggested.

"Or *backside,*" Malcolm said. "But that's not very scientific."

"Gooney Bird?" Mrs. Pidgeon asked. "You're the one with the photographic memory. What did the book say?"

Gooney Bird was able to remember things by seeing them in her mind as if she were looking at a photograph. With her eyes closed, she took several deep breaths in and out. Then she reopened her eyes and said, "It just showed the big muscle and told its official name.

*Gluteus maximus.* There was an arrow pointing to it and the label said it was the biggest muscle but it didn't say the name of the body part it was pointing to.

"Of course," she added, "it was pointing to the butt."

"Well," said Mrs. Pidgeon after a moment. "Let's leave it."

"Good!" Tyrone said. "Because I was already making up a rap. And it goes: *Hey, Napoleon, you know what? Your biggest muscle be right in your butt!*" He placed his hands on his own behind and wiggled his hips.

"We could do a whole show! We could do a show with raps about body parts! We could sell tickets! I bet we could make a lot of money!" Malcolm was dancing with excitement. "And it could be called, ah, *The Body Show*! Or maybe—"

"I know! I know!" Chelsea called. We could call it—"

She was interrupted by the ringing of a bell

and the intercom announcement that it was time to line up for school buses.

"Yikes! We'd better go get our coats!" Barry said.

The second-graders waved to Napoleon, smiling toothy grins at him, and hurried from the gym.

8

Unfortunately Mrs. Pidgeon's prediction had come true. By the time Napoleon had been in the gym for several days, Mrs. Gooch had telephoned Mr. Leroy six times to complain about what she called a "bad word." She meant *butt.*

On Thursday the second-graders crumpled up the sign that told about the largest muscle and threw it away.

"We could make another sign that says the name of that big muscle," Tricia suggested.

"What was it, Gooney Bird?"

"*Gluteus maximus.* It's Latin," Gooney Bird said.

"We could put that on his butt sign."

"Or," Gooney Bird pointed out, "we could say Napoleon's *derrière.* That's French for 'butt.'"

"But then Mrs. Gooch would say we were being un-American. She thinks everything is un-American," Chelsea said.

"Like what?" Malcolm asked. He found a wastebasket in the corner of the gym and tossed the crumpled sign into it.

"Spaghetti," Chelsea said.

"*Spaghetti?* That's everybody's favorite! How can it be un-American?"

Chelsea shrugged. "It's Italian. And also: french fries. She thinks we shouldn't eat french fries because they're French."

"So she'd *really* object to *derrière,*" Mrs. Pidgeon said with a sigh. "And by the way, the real reason we shouldn't eat french fries is because they're very greasy."

Malcolm looked worried. "What about hot dogs? Are they American?"

"German," Mrs. Pidgeon told him. "*Frank-furters*. They originated in Germany.

"I think ketchup is American, though," she added.

"You know what?" Beanie said. "We could have told all about that when we did Napoleon's digestive system. We could have said that he eats French food and German food—"

"And Italian food—" Barry added.

"And Japanese food—" Keiko said.

"And ketchup—" Malcolm said.

"Yes! Because all of us have the same kind of insides," Gooney Bird said. "It doesn't matter what country we come from."

"We're all alike," Felicia Ann said in her small voice, with a tiny smile.

"Speaking of Napoleon," Mrs. Pidgeon pointed out, "it's time to move him to his next location. Roll his stand over here. Barry and

Nicholas, can you take his sneakers off very carefully? And, Ben, put the basketball over there in the corner with the others. We'll have to dress him in a new outfit and make some new signs for . . . Who remembers?"

Everyone did. "Respiratory System!" they shouted.

They rolled Napoleon back to the second grade classroom and began to prepare him for his next demonstration. On Monday the skeleton would be going outside for the first time.

The lion part of March—the very cold and blustery part—was ending. It was a little warmer, though there was still some old snow on the ground. Very small buds had appeared on some of the bushes. They could tell that spring was coming. Tricia said that she had seen a robin.

But it was still chilly. They wrapped a warm scarf around Napoleon's neck and pulled a knitted blue hat over his skull.

"He should have gloves," Felicia Ann suggested. But they all looked at his long bony hands and agreed that it would be too difficult to fit gloves on him.

"Anyway, he wouldn't be able to hold his cigarette if he has gloves on," Nicholas pointed out.

"No!" the other children shouted. They had been arguing with Nicholas all day. Nicholas thought it would be a good idea to explain the respiratory system by showing Napoleon smoking.

"See, he goes outside to have a cigarette. My dad does that at work," Nicholas said. "He stands out on the sidewalk and smokes. Then we can make signs saying how the smoke goes in Napoleon's lungs and makes them all black and yucky, so he shouldn't do it."

"Nicholas," Mrs. Pidgeon had said, "we've already had a complaint because we gave him a wineglass—"

"And because we talked about his butt," Malcolm reminded everyone.

"Right," Mrs. Pidgeon continued. "So we are *not* going to give Napoleon a cigarette! No way. Instead we are going to demonstrate how healthy it is for him to be outside breathing in the fresh spring air."

"But what can we give him to hold? He had a basketball for Muscular System. He had a fork for Digestive System. And he had a book for Brain."

"I know!" Tricia said. "He can have my inhaler. He can have asthma!"

"I don't think so, Tricia," Mrs. Pidgeon said. "You might need it, sweetie."

"I know!" Gooney Bird said suddenly. She lifted the top of her desk, rummaged around, and brought something out. "Here!" she said. "Left over from a birthday party I went to!"

"Balloons!" the second-graders said. "Napoleon can blow up a balloon!"

"With his *lungs!*" Tyrone said. "Cool!"

On Monday afternoon, Mrs. Pidgeon and

the children put on their own jackets. Napoleon was already dressed. Tyrone and Felicia Ann carried the signs they had made, and a roll of tape. Carefully, quietly, they wheeled the skeleton down the hall and through the back door of the school. They had decided to arrange Napoleon on the back steps so that no one would see them. They could invite the other classes to come group by group in the morning to learn about the respiratory system. Mr. Leroy had promised to announce it on the intercom after the Pledge of Allegiance.

Malcolm and Barry each blew up one of Gooney Bird's balloons as they walked. When they were situated outside, with Napoleon seated comfortably on the back steps, they placed one balloon in his left hand, and the other between his teeth, as if he were blowing air into it.

The first sign was taped to the stair railing behind Napoleon.

NAPOLEON IS OUTSIDE
TO ENJOY THE FRESH AIR.
IT IS GOOD FOR HIM.

On the step next to his left foot, they taped the second.

HE BREATHES AIR INTO HIS LUNGS.
THEN HE BREATHES IT OUT,
OR HE USES IT TO BLOW UP A BALLOON,
OR TO TALK OR SING.

"I can hold my breath for forty-seven seconds," Ben announced. "My cousin timed me in my uncle's swimming pool."

"You have good, strong lungs," Mrs. Pidgeon said. "Everybody? Breathe in and you can feel your chest move. Then hold your breath for a few seconds before you blow it out."

All of the children took a deep breath. Everyone but Ben blew it out again. Ben held his breath until his face turned bright pink, then let it out with a *whoosh*.

"Good," Mrs. Pidgeon said. "You all have great lungs. No smokers. I can tell."

Beside Napoleon's arm, they taped a third sign.

NAPOLEON DOES NOT SMOKE.
HE TAKES GOOD CARE OF HIS LUNGS.

"Now for the really informational one," Gooney Bird said, holding up the last sign. "Where shall I put it?"

"How about right on his chest? You could tape it to his ribs," Barry suggested.

Gooney Bird nodded. She leaned down and attached the last sign to Napoleon's ribs.

WHEN HE BREATHES,
THE AIR GOES DOWN HIS WINDPIPE
AND INTO HIS LUNGS.

THEN HIS BLOOD TAKES OXYGEN
TO ALL OF HIS BODY.
WITHOUT OXYGEN NAPOLEON WOULD
DIE.

"He's already dead," Chelsea pointed out. "He's a *skeleton*."

"Well," Gooney Bird said, "you know what? He seems alive to me. I feel as if he's a friend. Good old Napoleon!" She patted his arm.

Malcolm grinned. "I find that—"

"Don't you dare say it, Malcolm!" Mrs. Pidgeon warned.

Malcolm clamped his hand over his mouth. All of the children watched him. After a moment he slowly removed his hand. "Sorry," he said. "I almost couldn't control myself."

"Okay, everyone," Mrs. Pidgeon said. "Let's have a few good deep breaths of fresh air."

Together the second-graders stood on the back steps of the school next to Napoleon. They breathed in and out. The March air was

still cool enough that they could see little puffs of steam as the warm air left their lungs.

"Now how about a whistle?" Gooney Bird suggested. "That uses our lungs." She put two fingers to her mouth and gave a shrill whistle.

"Or a hum?" suggested Keiko. "Hmm-mmm . . ."

"A scream?" said Chelsea. She took a deep breath and gave a loud scream. Everyone jumped.

"A whisper!" Felicia Ann suggested. All of the children smiled.

"Whisper whisper whisper," they said in low voices.

"A groan!" said Ben, and he groaned.

"A grunt!" Beanie said, and she grunted like a pig.

"A gasp!" Nicholas suggested.

"A sigh!" Tyrone sighed loudly.

Finally Mrs. Pidgeon said, "A song. Let's use our lungs and sing a song for Napoleon before we go in to do our math."

"I know just the one!" Gooney Bird started the song. *"You are my sunshine, my only sunshine—"* she sang.

All of the children joined in. They sang the entire song while they stood beside Napoleon, who sat on the steps, grinning, with a blue balloon in his mouth and a yellow one in his left hand.

They changed one word. *"Please don't take my skeleton away,"* they sang.

But someone did. The next morning, the back steps of Watertower Elementary School were empty. Napoleon was gone.

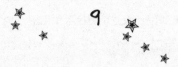

9

Everyone stood very still and stared at the step where they had left Napoleon, as if he might magically reappear. But there was no sign of him. Mrs. Pidgeon looked horrified.

Felicia Ann, Keiko, Beanie, and Malcolm all began to cry. Then Tyrone shoved Malcolm and called him a crybaby. Malcolm punched Tyrone in the arm and Tyrone began to cry.

"Call 911!" shouted Barry.

"Get Mr. Leroy!" shouted Chelsea.

All of the children yelled out suggestions until finally Mrs. Pidgeon, who still looked shocked, raised her arms and ordered them to quiet down. Gradually the noise subsided, though Malcolm stealthily kicked Tyrone in the ankle. Mrs. Pidgeon separated the boys. "Children," she said, "we have a serious problem and we must decide how to handle it. Of course we'll notify the principal.

"But first," she suggested, "everyone look around. Could Napoleon be someplace in the playground? Maybe someone moved him as a joke."

The children shaded their eyes against the bright sunlight and scanned the playground.

Nothing. No skeleton. Just the empty playground, a few trees with some very early buds, and a blue car driving slowly past, toward the stop sign at the corner. Keiko began to cry again, quietly. She wiped her nose on the sleeve of her jacket.

"My blue hat is gone too!" Nicholas wailed.

After a moment Gooney Bird climbed to the top of the steps and looked down to where all the dismayed second-graders were standing.

"Everyone!" she called out. "We have a crime to solve, and if it's okay with you, I'm going to appoint myself head detective, because Napoleon belongs to my Uncle Walter and I'm sort of responsible for him."

"Yeah, you might have to pay for him!" Barry said.

"I bet he cost about a thousand dollars!" Chelsea added.

"We could have a bake sale," Malcolm suggested.

"Children, let's not get ahead of ourselves," Mrs. Pidgeon said. "Let's concentrate on finding Napoleon. Does everyone agree that Gooney Bird should be head detective? We'll vote. All in favor, say *aye*."

"AYE!" the second-graders shouted.

"Thank you." Gooney Bird adjusted her hat. Today she was wearing a jester's cap with bells on it. "I'm kind of sorry I'm wearing my jester's cap today, because there isn't anything funny about this situation. If I'd known we would have a mystery to solve, I would have worn my Sherlock Holmes hat.

"But," she added, "that's the thing about mysteries. They take you by surprise."

"A bad surprise," Malcolm said in a gloomy voice.

"Yes," Gooney Bird agreed. "This is a bad surprise. But we're going to investigate in an orderly way. First we're going to check on the obvious suspect. Barry?"

*"Me?"* Barry said. "Why am I a suspect?"

"No, no, you're not. I'm sorry. I meant that I was appointing you to a task," Gooney Bird said. "I want you to go into the school and find Mr. Furillo."

"Mr. Furillo? Is *he* the suspect?" Mrs. Pidgeon asked. "Why on earth—?"

"Not him. His dog. Bruno. Barry, I want you to check on Bruno's whereabouts. Where was he when the crime was committed?"

Keiko sniffled and wiped her nose again.

"Why is Bruno a suspect?" she whimpered. "We all *love* Bruno!"

"Well," Gooney Bird said in a serious voice. "Bruno is a . . . what?"

"Dog," the children all replied.

"And we all know that Bruno is always hungry, correct?"

"Correct!" the children replied.

"And dogs like to eat—what?"

There was a silence. "Dog food?" Malcolm suggested in a hesitant voice.

But the children shook their heads. They knew what Gooney Bird meant. *"Bones,"* they said.

"And even though Mr. Furillo said that Bruno wouldn't be at all interested in Napoleon, still, Napoleon is . . . what?"

"Bones." The voices were very somber.

Mrs. Pidgeon cleared her throat. "Oh, dear," she said. "Maybe Bruno found that, ah, humerus."

Everyone was silent.

"Sorry," Mrs. Pidgeon murmured apologetically.

Then Barry said loudly, "Okay. I'm on the case. I'll find Mr. Furillo." He dashed up the steps and entered the school building.

"While Barry's gone," Gooney Bird announced, "we must all be looking carefully for clues. I'm sorry we don't have magnifying glasses. But search carefully."

All of the children looked at the ground. Ben poked a twig with his toe.

"No, no," said the head detective. "Spread out. We must search the steps and the walk and the playground."

"Is it okay, Mrs. Pidgeon?" Beanie asked. "It's not recess time."

Mrs. Pidgeon nodded. She looked at her watch. "It's actually spelling time. But for now this is more important. Start searching for clues."

The children began to wander the playground with their heads bent.

"Milky Way wrapper!" Malcolm called. "All crumpled up and very old!"

"Probably not a clue," Gooney Bird decided.

"Dirty mitten!" Chelsea called. "Looks like it was frozen and just melted recently!" She held up a soggy red object.

"Hey, is that mine? I lost a mitten at recess last month!" Nicholas ran over to take a look. "No," he said. "Kindergarten size."

"Broken pencil!"

"Dog poop!"

"Plastic toy from McDonald's!"

"Bubblegum wrapper!"

All of the children were finding things. They brought their findings, all but the dog poop, to Head Detective Gooney Bird, and she decided that none of them was a clue. Looking at each object, she shook her head. The bells on her jester's hat rang again and again.

Barry reemerged from the back door of the school with Mr. Furillo by his side. Behind them, Bruno ambled down the steps. His tail was still bandaged but he wagged it slightly. Mr. Furillo looked worried.

"Bruno's innocent," he said. "I'm quite sure. He went home with me last evening and he came to school with me this morning. He hasn't left my side."

Barry nodded. "Bruno has a witness," he said, "and an alibi."

"Good," Gooney Bird said. "I didn't want Bruno to be guilty."

The children and Mrs. Pidgeon all agreed. Bruno was a much-loved dog.

"But I really wish we could solve the crime." Gooney Bird sighed. She looked out over the playground. Nothing had changed. Out in the street, for the third time, the same blue car passed slowly again.

"Barry!" Gooney Bird said suddenly. "Write

down that car's license number! It keeps driving past. That's suspicious!"

Barry always had a Magic Marker in his pocket. Quickly he pulled it out, peered toward the car, and wrote the numbers on the back of his hand. "What should we do with the number?" he asked.

"I'm not sure. But on TV they always try to get the license number. Could you see who was driving?"

The children shook their heads.

"A woman, I think," Mrs. Pidgeon said.

"Was she wearing my blue hat?" Nicholas asked.

"I don't think so, Nicholas. Sorry." Mrs. Pidgeon put her arm around Malcolm.

"Kids," she said, "we'd better go back inside. We've done everything we can out here. Isn't that so, Gooney Bird?"

Gooney Bird frowned. She nodded. "I guess so. Here: I'll throw the useless clues away." She gathered the broken toys, the soggy mitten, and the scraps of paper that the children had collected. Then, while her classmates climbed the stairs to return to the building, she took the little pile of things to the trash can by the corner of the building. They all stood by the door and watched her. She looked dejected.

But when Gooney Bird lifted the lid of the large can, the look on her face changed. The bells on her jester's hat jingled as she looked up at the class. "Here's your hat, Nicholas!" she called. She leaned forward, reached into the can, and held up the knitted hat.

"And the scarf! Whose scarf was this?" Gooney Bird held up the plaid scarf that had been tied around Napoleon's neck.

"Mine!" Chelsea called. "Yay!"

"Is Napoleon in there, all folded up?" Barry asked.

"Nope. But wait—" Gooney Bird leaned forward, reaching into the big can. "Look!" she called, and held up the two balloons. They had lost some air and begun to deflate.

Standing there while the class watched her, Gooney Bird examined the hat, the scarf, and the two limp balloons. She held them each close to her face with a puzzled look.

Suddenly she grinned and looked up.

"I've solved the crime!" she announced loudly. "Now we just have to get Napoleon back!"

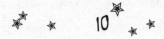

Back in the classroom, Gooney Bird passed around the hat, the scarf, and the two limp balloons. The objects went from desk to desk. Each child sniffed them. Some of the children made a face. "Yuck," Malcolm said loudly.

Tricia said, after she sniffed, "Yikes! I might need my inhaler!"

"Are we all in agreement about who stole Napoleon?" Gooney Bird asked.

Everyone nodded.

Mrs. Pidgeon frowned. "It certainly smells like Mrs. Gooch's perfume, that's true. Over-the-top gardenia."

"And she's the one who hates Napoleon," Beanie pointed out.

"But we don't really, truly have *proof*," Barry said, with a worried look. He stared down at the numbers written on the back of his hand. *7508J.*

"I have an idea," Gooney Bird said. "Veronica Gooch is in third grade, right?"

Everyone nodded.

"Well," Gooney Bird said, "we could try this." She described her plan.

"I think perhaps we should talk to Mr. Leroy," Mrs. Pidgeon said, after a moment.

"I'll put on my formal meeting hat," Gooney Bird said. Carefully she arranged her flowered hat over her red hair. Then she put on her white gloves and set out, with Mrs. Pidgeon's permission, for the principal's office. She was carrying the clues.

Seated behind his big desk, Mr. Leroy listened carefully to Gooney Bird's description of the kidnapping of Napoleon. He looked very concerned.

Carefully he sniffed the hat, gloves, and balloons.

"I agree," he said. "That's Mrs. Gooch's perfume. She's been in this office several times in the past few weeks, complaining about the skeleton. Her scent is very distinctive. I've had to spray air freshener in here again and again. My secretary always says, 'We've been Gooched.'"

"And we think it was Mrs. Gooch driving past in a blue car, watching us, when we discovered Napoleon was missing. We got the license number. Barry has it written on his hand. *7508J*. She kept going around the block really slowly," Gooney Bird explained. "She was probably even *laughing*," she added angrily.

Mr. Leroy stroked his necktie while he thought about the situation. Today he was wearing a tie with Jack-in-the-boxes on it. Jack had a silly smile on his face. But Mr. Leroy didn't. He looked very serious.

"And you said you have a suggestion?" he asked.

"Well, I'm the head detective. And we need proof that she is the thief. We have her perfume, of course." Gooney Bird wrinkled her nose and gestured to the little pile of objects on Mr. Leroy's desk. "But now we need to find out if that was her car driving sneakily past, watching us.

"So here is my idea. You get on the intercom and announce that you are holding a contest."

"A contest?" Mr. Leroy said.

"Yes. You tell everybody you're wondering how many children in the school know their parents' car license plate numbers. You can say it's a test of observation and memory. Tell all the children to write down the numbers. With their names, of course.

"Then you collect all of those from all the

classes and we look through the third grade ones to see if Veronica Gooch wrote down 7508J. And if she did? Ta da! We know it was her mom driving past."

Mr. Leroy was silent for a moment. Then he opened a drawer of his desk and removed a folder with a blue cover.

"You know what, Gooney Bird?" he said. "You are a wonderful detective. And I always enjoy your hats."

"Thank you," Gooney Bird said, arranging her flowered hat more tidily on her head. "I should be wearing my Sherlock Holmes hat. But I didn't know we'd have a mystery to solve today. So I am wearing my important meeting hat."

"Well, this is certainly an important meeting," the principal told her. "And you came up with quite a complex and effective way of identifying our suspect."

"Thank you."

"But the contest you describe would be quite time-consuming. And I think I can accomplish the same thing in about two minutes."

"You can?" Gooney Bird looked very interested. "How?"

Mr. Leroy opened his folder, turned a couple of pages, and ran his finger down a list until he found what he was looking for. Then he reached for his telephone and dialed the number he had located.

"Hello?" he said pleasantly, after a moment. "Mrs. Gooch? This is John Leroy."

Back in the second grade classroom, Gooney Bird removed her hat and gloves and returned them to her cubby. She smoothed her hair. Mrs. Pidgeon and the students were waiting.

"She has confessed," Gooney Bird announced.

The children clapped their hands.

"Mr. Leroy told her that if she didn't return

Napoleon immediately, he would have to notify the authorities."

"But is he okay?" asked Barry in a worried voice.

Gooney Bird nodded. "He's in her car trunk. The blue car. 7508J. Mr. Leroy told her that if he was broken, she might have to pay for him. So she got all flustered and said that she had bent his legs and arms pretty carefully. So he's not damaged."

"Thank goodness," said Mrs. Pidgeon.

"She *also* said," Gooney Bird told the class, "that he is disgusting, and after she returns him this afternoon, she hopes never to see him again in this school. And she would like all books about the human body removed from the school library."

The children gasped. They began to mutter. "That's not fair!" "He's not disgusting!" "She can't take books out of our library!" "What did Mr. Leroy say?"

"Mr. Leroy said we shouldn't worry. He said first of all, let's make sure we get Napoleon back and that he isn't damaged. Then he and Mrs. Clancy will talk to Mrs. Gooch and explain about how a library works and how important it is to have books about *everything,* and how it isn't her job to decide what other people can read."

Mrs. Pidgeon, who had been sitting at her desk, stood up and turned to the chalkboard. "Thank you, Gooney Bird," she said. "And now we have to get busy on our spelling. Our detective work took a lot of time, and we don't want to fall behind." She wrote the letter *H* on the board.

"But, Mrs. Pidgeon!" Chelsea called out. "We hadn't finished with all the lessons we were teaching the other kids about the human body! We still have more to do, when we get Napoleon back!"

Mrs. Pidgeon nodded. She wrote the letter *E* beside the *H.*

"We haven't done the liver, or the pancreas, or the spleen—" Ben said. He pointed to the poster with the outlined body and all its organs.

Gooney Bird interrupted him. "And I have bad news," she said. "Look at the calendar. Uncle Walter needs Napoleon back on Monday. We're not going to have time to do every single organ."

Mrs. Pidgeon wrote the letter A. She turned to the class. "You're right," she said. "We only have a limited time left with Napoleon. We'll do just one more very important exhibition with him for the school."

"Liver?" asked Ben. "Spleen?"

"Pancreas?" asked Beanie. "Or kidneys?"

"Skin!" Tricia called out. "My mom said our skin is our biggest organ. And she should know because she's a dermatologist! That's a skin doctor."

"How about appendix?" Malcolm asked. "When I had a stomachache last summer, my dad thought it might be my appendix. But it wasn't. It was just that I sneaked a whole entire bag of cheese puffs at a picnic and ate every single one, and then had ice cream. After I threw up, my stomachache disappeared."

Mrs. Pidgeon chuckled. "Malcolm, Malcolm, Malcolm," she said.

"Appendix isn't an *organ*," muttered Berry.

Gooney Bird raised her hand politely. "If we're only doing one more part of Napoleon, it should be a really important part."

"I agree," said Mrs. Pidgeon. "Of course all the parts of the body are important. They all do their work together. And while you children have been thinking about which part of Napoleon we'll use for our final exhibition, none of you noticed that I was about to use the most important part for one of our spelling words." She reached for the chalk. The children looked carefully at what she had written on the board.

*HEA*

"Head!" Barry called.

"Head?" said Tricia. "But we already did the brain!"

"We could put a big hat on him, though, or maybe a wig," Chelsea suggested, "and then we could maybe talk about his hair, and— and—?"

Felicia Ann said, in her small voice, "I don't think *head* will be very interesting."

Mrs. Pidgeon smiled and added another letter to the board. Now it said *H E A R*

"Hearing?" asked Keiko. "But we already talked about how we hear when we did the brain."

Gooney Bird was grinning. "Everybody!" she called. "Close your eyes and listen to this!"

All of the children closed their eyes and sat quietly.

In a soft, mysterious voice, Gooney Bird said, "Thu-dump, thu-dump, thu-dump. Put your hands on your chests."

The second-graders, with their eyes tightly closed, put their hands on their chests as if they were saying the Pledge of Allegiance.

"Thu-dump, thu-dump."

The children, with their hands still on their chests, all opened their eyes. They were smiling.

*"Heart!"* they said, and Mrs. Pidgeon added the final letter to the word.

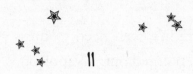

11

"March is finally like a lamb, not a lion!" Mrs. Pidgeon pointed out as the children streamed onto the playground wearing only sweaters: no hats, mittens, earmuffs, or parkas. Spring was here at last. The sun was shining and the willow tree at the corner of the playground had turned pale green.

Napoleon had been returned to them safely, and now they edged the skeleton, dangling from his stand, down the front steps. It was his final day at Watertower Elementary School.

"We didn't even need to dress Napoleon," Malcolm pointed out. "Napoleon is *naked!*"

Keiko squealed and put her hands over her ears. "Don't say 'naked,'" she said.

"He's not wearing clothes, but he's wearing gardenia perfume," Chelsea pointed out, wrinkling her nose.

"I'll have to explain to Uncle Walter that Napoleon got Gooched," Gooney Bird said. "It will wear off."

"Is Dr. O. here yet?" Barry asked, looking around.

"No. But he will be," Gooney Bird told him. "No one in my family is ever, ever late.

"Look! There are my parents, over there." She waved. Her mom, who had long pigtails and was wearing army boots, waved back.

"Mine too!" said Chelsea.

"And my mom," sighed Malcolm, "with the babies." He waved to a woman standing beside a huge stroller.

"And mine!" Tyrone said, grinning at his mom and dad. *"There they be, standing by the fence,"* he chanted. *"The brothers and the sisters and the triplets and the 'rents!"*

The second grade parents, who had been invited to Napoleon's final lesson and farewell, were all standing together at the edge of the playground, smiling.

Mr. Leroy, the principal, came down the front steps of the school. He greeted the parents.

"Ready, Gooney Bird?" he asked.

Today Gooney Bird was wearing a men's felt hat, the kind of hat that she said was called a fedora. "When I have a daughter someday," she had once said, "I am thinking of naming her Fedora. It has a nice sound to it."

Now she nodded. "Ready. I'll just pass these out to the parents." She was holding a stack of papers that she had prepared that morning, in Mr. Leroy's office. Carefully she distributed them to the audience. Then she gave one to Mr. Furillo, who was standing with Bruno near the door.

"Where's Uncle Walter?" she asked her parents. "No one in our family is ever, ever late!"

"He's on his way," Gooney Bird's father explained. "He called a few minutes ago. He had car trouble. He said to start without him."

Mrs. Pidgeon began the ceremony. "This is Napoleon," she said to the gathering of parents. "He has been visiting our school since the beginning of March, but today is his last day with us. Gooney Bird has given each of you a picture. Now she's going to explain what you are looking at."

Gooney Bird went to the top of the steps and adjusted her hat. Her wrist jingled. "I am wearing my charm bracelet," she told everyone. "I wear it on special occasions, like today. And this morning I used the copying machine in Mr. Leroy's office, and I copied my charm bracelet so that you could each see it up close. Take a look."

The parents and Mr. Furillo all looked carefully at the papers they were holding. There was a picture of Gooney Bird's bracelet with all its small silver charms.

"We're going to use the charms to tell you about what we've been learning about the human body. Napoleon has been helping us. Chelsea is going first. Chelsea?"

Gooney Bird took off her fedora and placed it on Chelsea's head as she stepped forward.

"First charm is a skull," Chelsea said in a loud voice. They had all practiced using outdoor voices. "Sometimes skulls look scary. But they shouldn't. This is Napoleon's head. And he is smiling. And also he took very good care of his teeth. Everybody? Smile like Napoleon!"

All of the children, and the parents, and Mr. Leroy, and Mr. Furillo, gave big smiles that showed their teeth. The only ones not smiling were Bruno, who was chewing on a stick, and the triplets, who were asleep in their stroller.

Chelsea removed the fedora and gave it to Ben, who came forward and put it on.

"Napoleon's skull is protecting his brain," Ben explained. "If you look at the charm bracelet, you can see how when we took him to the library and learned about his brain, Napoleon sat in a rocking chair, wearing glasses and reading a book."

All of the parents, looking at the pictures they were holding, smiled as they identified the chair, the spectacles, and the book.

"He was using his brain for all of that," Ben pointed out. Then he bowed, and removed the fedora. "Malcolm? You're next," he said.

Malcolm put on the fedora. "Next," he announced, "find the lobster and the wineglass and the pizza slice."

The parents all nodded, after they had located those charms on their pictures.

"We learned about digestion from

Napoleon," Malcolm continued. "We had to take away his wineglass because someone named Mrs. Gooch got all upset and—"

Mrs. Pidgeon put her hand on Malcolm's shoulder. "I don't think we need to talk about Mrs. Gooch," she murmured.

"Well, anyway, when Napoleon was drinking and eating the lobster and the pizza, everything got mixed with saliva and went down his esophagus, and then it churned around and turned into moosh in his stomach, and after that the moosh went into his intestines, and . . ."

"I think you can stop there, Malcolm," Mrs. Pidgeon whispered.

"Can I say about the toilet?" Malcolm asked.

"No," Mrs. Pidgeon said firmly. "Who's next?"

"Me!" Barry came forward and put the fedora on. "Next, after he ate, Napoleon went to the gym."

"First he went to the bathroom," Malcolm muttered.

Barry ignored Malcolm. He continued. "Look at the sneaker and the basketball. When he was in the gym, we all learned about Napoleon's muscles. His muscles make his bones move. Without muscles, we would just be like statues."

Tricia put up her hand, suddenly. "Excuse me for interrupting," she said. "But without *skin,* we would be a *blob.* Our skin holds all of our insides together. Isn't that right, Mom?"

She looked over at the parents. Tricia's mom waved and smiled. "That's right," she said.

"My mom is a dermatologist," Tricia explained.

"May I continue?" Barry asked in an irritated voice.

"Sorry," Tricia said.

"Back to muscles," Barry continued. "Muscles work in pairs." He held up his arm.

"One muscles stretches it out, the other muscle pulls it back." He demonstrated.

"Good job, Barry," Mrs. Pidgeon said. "Who's next?"

"Wait," Barry said, "I just want to say one more thing! It is okay to eat the other kind of mussels, because they are not spelled the same."

"Me! I'm next!" Felicia Ann stepped forward and reached for the fedora. She put it on her own head. It was too big and slipped over her eyes, but Felicia Ann didn't mind.

"Big voice, Felicia Ann," Mrs. Pidgeon reminded her.

Felicia Ann nodded, and the fedora slipped down farther over her face. She shouted, "The reason I'm able to shout is because of the air in my lungs! Napoleon's ribs protect his lungs because they are very important! All of his cells need oxygen, and they get it from his lungs!

"If you look at the charm bracelet, you'll see

a pipe. If Napoleon smoked a pipe, it would damage his lungs! So don't do that! Or cigarettes, either!"

"That means you, Dad!" Nicholas said loudly.

His father, standing in the audience, looked guilty. "Got it, son," he said. "I'm trying to quit."

Felicia Ann lifted the fedora off. "You know what?" she said to the other second-graders. "When I can't *see* anything, I'm not so shy!" She grinned.

Gooney Bird replaced the fedora on her own head. "There are two more charms on the bracelet," she announced. "The first one is a little heart. Nicholas and Beanie are going to pass around some hearts for you."

Nicholas and Beanie, each carrying a small bag, distributed red cinnamon hearts to everyone. Mr. Furillo nodded okay when they got to Bruno, so Bruno got a cinnamon heart as well, but it made him sneeze.

"Napoleon's heart is there behind his ribs,

between his lungs, and without it, Napoleon would be dead.

"Well, he is dead, actually. He's a skeleton. But you know what I mean. Our hearts are very, very important because they pump our blood around, and our blood carries oxygen to all our cells, and that's what keeps our organs working.

"And we make valentines shaped like hearts, and we say I HEART New York and other stuff, because some people think we feel love inside our hearts.

"Personally," Gooney Bird continued, "I think we probably feel love in our brains and in our muscles and in our bones and in our stomachs. Maybe even our liver. But we didn't have time to study the liver."

"Or pancreas," Malcolm added.

"Or spleen," said Barry.

"There is one more charm on the bracelet, and it's a Volkswagen Beetle. You can just ignore that one because it doesn't have anything to do with Napoleon," Gooney Bird explained.

"You can come up one by one and shake Napoleon's hand if you want to, and tell him goodbye. We're going to miss him. But my Uncle Walter needs him back."

"Just a minute!" Dr. Oglethorpe, wearing a suit and tie, suddenly came jogging up the walkway that led from the school parking lot. "Sorry I'm late!"

He introduced himself to all of the parents. "I'm out of breath from hurrying," he said. "Huffing and puffing! But you already know about the lungs, right?"

Nicholas's father groaned. "I *said* I'm quitting!"

"I'm gonna bug you, Dad," Nicholas said.

Dr. Oglethorpe turned to Napoleon and smiled as if he were greeting an old friend. Then he sniffed. "What . . . ?"

Gooney Bird explained quickly, in a low voice. "He got Gooched. It will wear off."

*"Gooched?"* Dr. Oglethorpe whispered.

"I'll explain later," Gooney Bird whispered back.

Dr. Oglethorpe lifted Napoleon's right arm and bent the wrist back and forth so that Napoleon seemed to wave. "I imagine he'll be sorry to leave the school," he said. "I bet he has had a lot of adventures here!"

The children nodded. "He read a book and ate and drank and played basketball and blew up balloons," Barry said.

"And he got stolen," Malcolm added.

*"Stolen?"* Dr. Oglethorpe repeated. He looked down at the long bone in Napoleon's arm. "I find this humerus," he said.

Everyone groaned.

"Okay," Dr. Oglethorpe said. "I agree. Dumb joke. You know what is going to be humorous, though? Watching me drive away with Napoleon, because when my car broke down

I had to borrow my neighbor's. We'll have to fold Napoleon carefully at his joints and he'll sit beside me in a tiny VW Beetle on the way home."

"Ta-da!" Gooney Bird said, and jingled her charm bracelet.